BUILDER BATTLE

Text by Thomas Kingsley Troupe

Illustrated by Alan Brown

raintree

a Capstone company — publishers for children

Raintree is an imprint of Capstone Global Library Limited, a
company incorporated in England and Wales having its registered
office at 264 Banbury Road, Oxford, OX2 7DY – Registered
company number: 6695582

www.raintree.co.uk
myorders@raintree.co.uk

Designed by Dina Her
Cover art by Fran Bueno
Image credit: Shutterstock: Elena_Lapshina, (pixel texture) design
element

978 1 3982 5389 6

British Library Cataloguing in Publication Data
A full catalogue record for this book is available from the
British Library.

Printed and bound in India.

CONTENTS

MAIN PLAYERS

SAMUEL FINNEGAN

JAMIE ANDERSON

MOLLY PETRENKO

CHAPTER 1

BYE-BYE BRIDGE

An undead groan came from somewhere in the distance. Then another. They were getting closer.

"Ghouls," Samuel Finnegan whispered. "It's always ghouls."

He immediately dropped what he was building and ran to the edge of the chasm. He'd planned on rebuilding the bridge later when he could spend more time on it. Knowing the monstrous army was coming, time was something he no longer had.

Samuel started to run across his bridge, and a smile spread across his face.

Well, I was going to tear this thing down anyway, he thought. He got to work.

As he ran the connections to the trigger on the castle side of his bridge, he looked up at his enormous creation. Castle Finnegan was beautiful beneath the perfect blue sky. Big, fluffy digital clouds drifted by.

Samuel loved his castle. It had taken him almost a month to build it, and he was extremely proud of the engineering he'd put into its construction. There were hidden rooms, trapdoors and a vault where he kept all of his precious building materials. It was –

Another groan. The ghouls were closer.

Snap out of it, Sam, he warned himself. *They're coming.*

Moving quickly, he placed the charges on the underside of the bridge and connected them to each other. Seeing that it wasn't as perfect as he liked, he rerouted the wire so that each one would activate after the previous one.

"If you're going to do it, do it right," Samuel whispered to himself. It was something his grandma told him and his brother, Ricky, time and time again. "You're right, Grandma."

As he spotted the first of the ghouls coming up the hill, Samuel made the connection. They shambled towards his bridge, moving in unison. Samuel did a quick monstrous head count. There were at least fifteen of them. All looked identical, all wanting nothing more than to eat his face.

Not today, fellas, Samuel thought.

The first few ghouls stepped onto the bridge, groaning and making noise as they got closer. He supposed they could smell him, making them even hungrier by the second.

"C'mon, you grot-bags," Samuel whispered. "Get on the bridge. Uncle Sam has something for you."

Samuel looked down. Everything was in

place. He had power, the connections were made, and all he had to do was step on the switch. He just wanted a few more on his bridge before the magic happened.

"And that's ten!" Samuel shouted as the foot of ghoul number ten stepped onto the wood. "Good enough."

Samuel stepped forwards and onto the switch. It clicked nice and loud before the blue light raced through the lines and towards his bridge. The first section exploded in a burst of pixels, dropping chunks of wood and ghoul into the deep chasm below. A minute later, the second charge erupted, followed by the third. In a matter of seconds, the old bridge to Samuel's castle was a smoking ruin.

On their way down, the ghouls' groans faded.

"Thanks for stopping by," Samuel said and smiled.

He turned and glanced up at his beautiful fortress again. Castle Finnegan was safe for now. The bridge, however, was another story.

A tap on his shoulder made him jump.

*   *   *

Samuel pulled off his headphones and looked away from his computer monitor.

"Bro," his younger brother Ricky said. "You're *still* playing that baby game?"

Samuel groaned and put down his headset.

"*Buildtopia* is *not* a baby game," Samuel said. "It's way too complex for most infants – maybe even you."

"Very funny," Ricky said, flopping onto Samuel's bed. "I just can't believe you're still playing something that looks like that. Especially when there are so many games out there with better graphics. And, you know, games where you don't have to *build* everything."

"I like building stuff," Samuel admitted with a shrug. "It relaxes me. Plus, I've been playing this for years. There's some nostalgia there."

"Yeah," Ricky said. "Or maybe you're just rubbish at real games."

With that, Samuel stood up and chased his little brother out of his room.

Ricky's door slamming shut and Mum yelling from the basement cut the chase short.

"What's going on up there, boys?"

"Nothing," Samuel called back. "Just Ricky being Ricky."

When Samuel went back to his room, he noticed a window had popped up on his monitor. He read the text above the progress bar.

Updating game. Please wait.

CHAPTER 2

GAME CHANGER

What's happening? Samuel wondered, feeling a little worried.

He watched as an update was downloading automatically. It had been years since anything new had been added to *Buildtopia*. None of his friends even talked about it any more. They had all moved on to bigger next-generation games.

Samuel paced around his room, wondering what they were doing to his beloved game. Would the update affect the worlds he'd already built?

Samuel glanced at the progress bar. It was almost complete. "Please don't ruin the game," he pleaded. "It's fine the way it is."

He could hear his old computer's fan kick in as the download completed and the latest update began to install. After a few minutes, his monitor blinked off as his computer restarted itself automatically.

Samuel dashed to his chair, sat down and waited. When the screen came back on, he relaunched the game immediately.

"Whoa," Samuel whispered. A smile crept across his face.

*　*　*

Samuel spent the next few hours looking over all of the updates to *Buildtopia*. The developers had fixed some long-standing glitches in the game. They had also given the graphics a slight visual update. But the biggest change to *Buildtopia* was the addition of online competitions.

After finishing his homework, Samuel spent a good chunk of his weekend trying out the new game modes. FORTRESS had players quickly build a fort to keep themselves and their villagers safe. BATTLE ROYALE pitted everyone against each other in a huge fight to see who would be the last survivor.

But Samuel's favourite mode was CAPTURE THE CROWN. It was played on an aerial battleground with four floating forts on the northern, southern, western and eastern ends. Each of the four forts had a crown inside. Long, thin bridges connected them together.

Teams of five competed against each other. When a crown was captured and returned to its home base, the team whose crown was stolen was eliminated. It was also game-over for any player who fell into the void below. The team with the most crowns or whoever survived the longest was the winner.

As a *Buildtopia* player for years, Samuel quickly discovered he was really good at the game. All of his training was paying off!

When he was added to a team of five, he moved like a pro to the forts, avoided the traps and arrows shot at him and brought crown after crown to his teammates.

"Nice one, ComicSams1006!" Dark-Hair-Dave, a player on Samuel's team, shouted through his headset. ComicSams1006 was Samuel's online name. "You've played before, eh?" Dark-Hair-Dave added.

"Oh, here and there," Samuel replied.

"Well, get ready," Dark-Hair-Dave said. "We've got a new team moving in."

Samuel got into position as the game started. Dave stayed back to guard the crown with Zoe#1inaMillyun and a few of the others. As the screen displayed *GO FORTH,* Samuel ran his character towards the northern fort. A player dressed all in black and a motorcycle helmet dashed across the bridge towards him.

Before Samuel could even react, the player fired an arrow. He hit Samuel's character in the forehead. The next moment, Samuel's character was falling off the bridge – eliminated for the first time.

YOU'RE OUT, the screen declared. Samuel looked at the screen in disbelief. He'd been playing for hours, and it was the first time he'd been knocked out. He watched the rest of the match unfold from the sidelines. The character in black's name displayed over their character.

TheArchitect2706.

Samuel watched TheArchitect2706 steal all of the crowns with little to no trouble. The game was over almost as soon as it had started.

"Oh, you're good," Samuel whispered to his screen.

CHAPTER 3

POPULAR AGAIN

Samuel had completely lost track of time when his mum came in his room. As she put her hand on his shoulder, he jumped. Mum jumped too, scared by his reaction.

"Ugh!" she cried. "This game is melting your brain."

"Sorry," Samuel said, taking off his headset. "They did some new stuff to the game, so I was –"

"Playing it all weekend," Mum finished. "I hope you finished your homework at least."

"Of course, Mum," Samuel replied. "I got it done on Friday after dinner."

"Well, get to bed," Mum said. "There's school tomorrow."

Samuel's mum kissed the top of his head before leaving the room.

Samuel sighed. He turned to his game and watched TheArchitect2706 destroy the competition yet again. Try as he might, he couldn't win against them.

"Nice game, whoever you are," Samuel said, logging off. He shook his head. Even though he'd played well, it seemed TheArchitect2706 was a bigger *Buildtopia* fan than he was.

* * *

At school the next morning, Samuel's best friend Benny ran over to his locker.

"Hi, Samuel," Benny said. "Looks like your old Building Nerds game is popular again."

Samuel shook his head. "First, it's *Buildtopia*. Get it right!" he replied. "Second . . . what are you talking about?"

Benny looked shocked. "Are you telling me you don't know about the update?"

Samuel nodded. "Oh, I know all about it," he said. "I was playing it all weekend after it dropped. How do *you* know about it?"

Benny smiled. "Everyone's talking about it."

"I find that really hard to believe, Ben," Samuel said. "It's a dead game, remember? Only builder geeks like me play it."

"Apparently not," Benny said. "Everyone is saying the game is getting its own esports competition. Jamie Anderson is already trying to form a team."

Samuel wondered if he was dreaming. How was it possible that his old favourite game was suddenly being talked about by someone as popular as Jamie Anderson? And an esport tournament?

"Seriously," Samuel whispered. "What is happening?"

"Simple, Sam," Benny replied. "Your game went from LAME-ous to FAME-ous."

Samuel shook his head. "*That* was lame, Benny."

During school that day, Samuel listened as loads of his classmates talked about *Buildtopia*. Some mentioned having to download the game again after deleting it years ago. Others talked about Jamie forming his esports team. In the corridor after lunch, Samuel overheard Jamie himself talking to a few of his friends.

"Yeah, I've been a big fan of the game since day one," Jamie bragged. "It seems only natural that I'd be the one to get a team from Prescott Middle School together."

Samuel had to cover his mouth with his hand to keep from laughing out loud. *Big fan since day one?* Before the weekend, there wasn't *anyone* in his school who played *Buildtopia* any more. At least no one that he knew about!

Leave it to Jamie to jump on the bandwagon, Samuel thought, listening a little more.

"I'll probably have trials so that I can have the best five people on my squad," Jamie said. "We'll destroy the competition."

As he listened to Jamie and his friends talk more, he wondered, *Did Jamie know how to build anything in the game? Could he construct a pressure trap? Could he build a rock-a-pult? Did he know how to perform jumbo jumps to get further distance and height?*

Samuel knew these and a hundred more tricks that only dedicated players were aware of. These weren't things you could just "do" after being out of the game so long.

Samuel decided right then and there that he would audition. He would show them all what they were missing from their team – a *Buildtopia* genius.

CHAPTER 4

TIRING TRIALS

In the week that followed, Samuel spent a lot of his free time playing CAPTURE THE CROWN in *Buildtopia*. More and more people were talking about it. By the time the *Buildtopia* creator Super Smile Games announced their regional esports tournament dates, the excitement went through the roof.

As Samuel was playing his twelfth round of CAPTURE THE CROWN that Friday night, he got a text from Benny.

Benny: *Trials for Jamie's squad are tomorrow @ 2. Birchview Leisure Centre. Don't be late!*

Samuel thought about that. He could get a lift from his mum and blow them away with his insane skills. He texted Benny back.

Samuel: *Perfect. Can anyone go?*

Benny: *Think so! But just so you know, he's calling the team Jamie's Juggernauts.*

Samuel groaned. He took a deep breath and responded.

Samuel: *That's terrible!*

Benny: *What did you expect?*

Samuel: *Thanks for the heads up.*

Benny: *GOOD LUCK TOMORROW!*

* * *

It took some convincing, but on Saturday afternoon, Samuel was in the passenger seat of his mum's car heading towards the Birchview Leisure Centre across town.

On the way there, he thought about all the tricks and techniques he was going to display for Jamie to see. By the time he had done his trial, there would be no other option than to have him join the team.

Nervously, Samuel checked the time. It was 1:47 pm, and they were still quite far from the leisure centre. "We're going to be late, Mum," Samuel said. "Can you maybe step on it?"

"This isn't like one of your video games, Sammy," Mum said.

Samuel groaned. He wished he could hop out, attach some blue energy to the tyres, route it to a controller and activate it. In *Buildtopia,* he could make anything float with the magic stuff. It would be much faster to rise up and float over the tops of the other cars.

He checked the time every few seconds. It seemed like every time he checked, the time jumped minutes closer to 2 pm. There was no way he'd get there before the trials started.

As his mother rounded the corner, there was an audible loud bang. A second later, the car started to rumble.

"Ah, that's just great!" his mother cried.

"What's wrong? What's happened?" asked Samuel.

"Flat tyre," Mum said.

* * *

Samuel stood on the pavement with his mum, looking helplessly at the car. His dreams of making it to the trials were disappearing as quickly as the air from their blown-out tyre.

"Well," Mum said, "let's get to work."

She opened the boot as Samuel looked down the street. The leisure centre was probably ten minutes away by foot. He could run there, do his thing and run back.

He turned to see Mum shifting things around in the boot. She lifted the panel that hid the temporary spare tyre.

"Mum, would it be okay if . . . ," Samuel started, gazing down the street again.

His mum looked up, her eyebrows raised, waiting for what was next.

I can't do it, Samuel decided right then and there, ". . . if I loosened the nuts on the tyre?"

His mum smiled and handed him the wrench. "Of course."

*   *   *

It took Samuel and his mum far too long to change the tyre. By the time they got the spare tyre on and were heading back down the road, it was closer to three o'clock than two. When Samuel ran into the leisure centre and found the room Jamie had set up for the trials, he heard clapping and cheering.

Jamie stood at the front of the room with four other kids from his school.

It had already been done. Jamie had already picked his Juggernauts for the esports team.

I'm too late, Samuel thought. *It's over.*

CHAPTER 5

CREEPY COMPETITOR

Samuel rode home with his mum in silence.

"I'm sorry, Samuel," Mum said, guiding the car into their driveway.

"It's not your fault, Mum," Samuel said. "Just bad luck, that's all."

"Maybe they can make room for you on the team?" Mum suggested.

Samuel smiled. "Yeah, it doesn't really work that way. It's a five-versus-five competition, so there's no room for a sixth."

Mum shook her head as she pulled into the garage. "I'll never understand all that video game stuff," she admitted. "But I'm sure you'll work something out."

When Samuel got to his room, he went through the list of Jamie's Juggernauts.

Jamie Anderson – sporting hero turned *Buildtopia* esports captain?

Molly Petrenko – a girl from his maths class who drew cartoons while taking notes. Not the *Buildtopia* type.

Tony Ahmadi – mellow guy who always has his head in a book and usually looks like he's having a bad day.

Jonah Jackson – big-time gamer who always has the latest and greatest gaming consoles and games. Made sense, but why play old *Buildtopia*? Just because everyone else is?

Sheva Abrams – a girl who is constantly creating content for her social media channel. Being on Jamie's Juggernauts will probably bring her even more followers.

It didn't help that Samuel missed watching them play during the trials. Who knows?

Maybe each of them boasted insane skills since the *Buildtopia* update.

His phone hummed. A text from Benny. The preview on his home screen said: *WELL?!?!?*

Samuel didn't feel like reliving the disappointment. He put his phone down without replying. Instead, he went to his computer and logged on to *Buildtopia*.

Within minutes, he was dropped into yet another round of CAPTURE THE CROWN.

Samuel pulled on his headset and talked to his randomly assigned teammates. He wished he had real friends who were into *Buildtopia*. Even after all the hype, Benny still had no interest in the game.

As the match started, he saw a familiar player dressed in black with a motorcycle helmet running across the bridge towards their fortress. It was TheArchitect2706!

"Watch this one, guys," Samuel ordered his teammates. He ran towards the opposing player and executed a jumbo jump, launching himself over The Architect's head. After he landed, he turned and began chipping away at the bridge – cutting off their escape.

You might get our crown, but you're not bringing it back home, Samuel thought.

The Architect knocked two of Samuel's team members into the abyss, quickly reducing them to a team of one. With no time to lose, Samuel built a platform on the other side of the bridge. Then he assembled a rock-a-pult and loaded it with explosive amber. He watched The Architect disappear into Samuel's team's fortress.

"Three, two, one," Samuel whispered. He unleashed the amber, watching the golden chunks fly towards the fort's entrance. As The Architect emerged, they were peppered with explosions.

THEARCHITECT2706 HAS BEEN ELIMINATED! the game announced.

"YES!" Samuel shouted. He ran over to the fallen opponent and retrieved the crown that lay by their side. Dodging arrows from the other teams, he ducked into his team's fortress and replaced it on the pedestal.

"We've got them on the run!" a teammate named DoggieBreathAZ shouted. "Let's gooooo!"

As Samuel turned to run back out into the battlefield, a message popped up on his screen in the lower right-hand corner.

His eyes widened as he saw who it was from: *TheArchitect2706.*

The message made him stop in his tracks. It simply said:

I KNOW WHO YOU ARE.

CHAPTER 6

WEARY WATCHER

"Okay, creepy," Samuel said as he finished the round. He found himself wondering who TheArchitect2706 was. And how did they know who he was? It wasn't like his profile name *ComicSams1006* spelled out his name or anything. And he knew better than to use his real name when playing online.

So who the heck are you? Samuel wondered. He took off his headset and sat back in his chair, thinking. It could be just some creep trying to scare him after finally being beaten.

Feeling hungry after his rubbish afternoon, Samuel headed downstairs for dinner and all but forgot about the strange message.

Samuel spent the rest of his weekend doing homework, playing the occasional game and watching videos on his phone. As he scrolled through his usual subscriptions, he noticed that Sheva Abrams had posted a new video on her channel she called SHEVA-VISION.

"Juggernauts' First Practice Sesh," Samuel read, rolling his eyes. "Give me a break."

Despite the urge to scroll on and watch something else, curiosity got the better of Samuel. He took a deep breath and hit play.

Sheva gave a quick introduction and explained the team and competition. Straight away, Samuel noticed the usernames for each player. *JJ-Jamie, JJ-Sheva, JJ-Tony, JJ-Molly, and JJ-Jonah.* The names were really boring, but it made it easy to follow who was who. He watched as Jamie's team played a round.

Tony ran across the first bridge towards the North fort while Jamie headed east. Sheva and Jonah stayed behind inside their South

fort, guarding the crown. Molly stood guard out front, knocking back anyone approaching – often into the pit.

"Okay, guys," Sheva's voice said over the video. "Here's where Tony totally blows it!"

Samuel watched as Tony ran into the North fort. Tony hoped to grab the crown and bring Jamie's Juggernauts their first point, eliminating Team North.

As soon as he came back out, two players jumped on him. One clobbered him with a digital club. The other one lifted Tony's red-cloaked avatar and threw him into the abyss.

"Ouch," Samuel whispered.

"Jamie's got the East fort's crown, and Jonah and I are ready to put the hurt on anyone that's chasing him," Sheva announced in her cheerful video voice.

Sure enough, Jamie came running across the bridge. An arrow or two hit him as he got closer to their home fort. As he reached the threshold, Molly's character leapt out from behind a wall and jumped over Jamie's head.

She ran at the three players from the East fort and kicked one into the pit. She built a wall in front of another and then backed up, deleting pieces of the bridge in front of her. As the player leapt over the wall, he fell into the void. The third player jumped up onto the wall, and Sheva shot at him with a volley of five arrows.

"Nice," Samuel said.

"That's teamwork, baby!" Sheva cried as Jamie ran into the fort and scored their first point. Team East was history.

Samuel watched as Jonah's character did a silly back-and-forth dance before defending their fort from the North fort's squad.

In seconds, Jonah and then Sheva were eliminated.

"Yeah, didn't see that one coming," Sheva admitted to her video-watching audience. "But it's all about the practice and team building. We'll get there!"

Samuel watched until the end of the video where Jamie and Molly were the last South players standing. In no time at all, their crown was stolen. Jamie chased after the thief. The thief had to be stopped before he could bring the crown back to their northern fort. It didn't happen, and the North team ended up winning the match 3–1.

When the video was over, Samuel threw his phone to the side and stared at the ceiling. He could think of 800 things he would've done differently. Besides Molly, no one else on the team was actually *building* anything.

If things didn't change, Jamie's Juggernauts didn't stand a chance in the tournament.

CHAPTER 7

TEAM TROUBLE

"You're quitting?!" Jamie Anderson shouted. His voice made the metal in the boy's locker room vibrate. "Are you serious!?"

Samuel looked up and saw Tony standing next to Jamie, his arms folded. He leaned against his locker with a blank expression on his face.

"Hello?" Jamie asked.

"Yes," Tony said. "You heard me right. I'm quitting. I don't like playing any more. And besides that? I'm sick of every mistake I make getting broadcast across the internet."

Samuel remembered the video he'd watched of Jamie's Juggernauts playing. He wasn't sure how many more Sheva had posted since then, but she wasn't exactly nice to Tony in her voice-overs.

"Great," Jamie said as Tony turned and walked away. "Thanks for leaving us hanging, Tony."

Benny slid in next to Samuel.

"Here's your big chance," Benny whispered.

"Nah, I'm alright," Samuel whispered back. "I'm sure he's got eighteen other people to pick from."

Samuel closed his own locker and watched Jamie stand there, shaking his head in anger. Some of his friends came over to calm him down, but he still seemed pretty angry.

"This is stupid," Jamie grunted, banging his fist against the locker. "Whatever. I'll find someone to take his spot by lunchtime and we'll . . . we'll be fine."

Samuel couldn't help but feel bad for the guy. Jamie didn't sound so sure.

Before he could do anything more,
Mr Dekanick told them to get moving and get
to the gym.

*   *   *

To Samuel, it seemed like there was nothing
else happening during the rest of the school
day except for the big scandal with Tony
and Jamie's Juggernauts. It was literally all
everyone was talking about.

*I'll be glad when lunch break is over and
everyone can just move on to something else,*
Samuel thought. *I don't want to hear about
any of this stuff any more, including Jamie's
Juggernauts.*

In the corridor before lunch, Samuel
stood at his locker and fished his lunch bag
out of his backpack. As he turned round, he
noticed Jamie and a swarm of his friends
coming down the corridor. They were all in
his ear about something. Samuel could only

guess they wanted to know who he'd picked to replace Tony.

Before Samuel could take a step towards the canteen, Molly Petrenko stopped him.

"You've got to be on the team," Molly said.

"Seriously?" Samuel replied. "What makes you say that?"

"You're really good," she said quickly. "I've seen you play."

Samuel looked at Molly like she'd fallen out of the sky.

"Thanks, but wait . . . how do you know –"

"Because I'm TheArchitect2706," she replied, cutting Samuel off.

CHAPTER 8

FRIENDLY FOE

"Are you kidding me?"

Samuel could hardly believe it. Molly Petrenko was The Architect!?

"Yeah," Molly admitted. "Sorry. I had no choice but to reveal my secret identity."

"I just had no idea that . . . you even played *Buildtopia*," Samuel said.

"I've been a builder from the beginning," Molly admitted.

The bell rang, signalling the beginning of lunch break.

"We need to get to the canteen," she said, tugging on Samuel's sleeve. "C'mon, before it's too late."

Samuel was too stunned to do anything else but follow. "How do you know I'm any good?" he asked as they passed through the double doors. "I've only beaten you once. You kicked my butt more times than I can count."

Molly smiled. "Yeah," she said, "Sorry about that. But I can tell you know what you're doing out there. We need someone like you who knows the mechanics and secrets of the game."

The two of them stopped in the crowded canteen as Molly looked around.

"Okay," she said finally. "Over there."

Samuel looked at where she was going and stopped.

"Wait a second," he said. "I'm not sure this is such a great idea."

Molly turned and looked Samuel in the eye. "What do you mean? You're good at *Buildtopia*, Tony left the team, we need someone who can help us on to victory and you're the guy for the job. Not only is it a great idea, it's the best idea. Seriously."

"Jamie probably already has someone else picked for the team," Samuel said.

"That's why we need to hurry," Molly said. "Before he does something stupid and picks one of his friends. You know, if you'd just come to the trials, this would've been much easier."

Samuel sighed. *If she only knew . . .*

As they approached Jamie, Samuel watched him stand up at the head of the table. He looked like he was about to give a speech.

"Okay, everyone," Jamie said, moving his hands as if to calm everyone down. "I've got an announcement to make."

Molly pulled Samuel through the gathered crowd until the two of them were next to Jamie. Immediately, Samuel felt himself go hot with embarrassment.

"Wait," Molly cried. "I've found our number five."

Jamie looked like someone had stepped on his foot.

"I've already –" Jamie began.

"Doesn't matter," Molly said. "Samuel is our guy. The dude is absolutely brilliant at *Buildtopia*."

"If he's so good, why wasn't he at the trials?" Jamie demanded, crossing his arms. He looked like an angry teacher, demanding that his students explain themselves.

"Yeah," Molly said, turning to Samuel. "Why weren't you?"

"I tried," Samuel admitted. "But my mum's car got a flat on the way there. By the time I came in, you'd already picked your team."

"Well, he's here now," Molly said. "And he's got old-school skills that we can definitely use on the team."

Jamie shook his head and studied Samuel, who felt like every pair of eyes in the canteen was watching him.

"I don't know," Jamie said.

Samuel nodded.

"I told you it was a stupid idea," Samuel said. "But, like, thanks anyway."

He turned and took a few steps away to find Benny and his usual lunch table.

"Wait," Jamie said. "Please, Samuel. We . . . we could use you."

Samuel stopped and gripped the top of his lunch bag tightly. He looked down at his feet for a moment before turning to face Jamie and Molly. Both of them – and the rest of the crowd – appeared to be waiting for his answer.

"Yeah," Samuel said. "Okay."

CHAPTER 9

IMPERFECT PRACTICE

Time seemed to race by for Samuel over the next week and a half. Jamie demanded that his Juggernauts practise as often as they could. He understood why he didn't see TheArchitect2706 online much after he'd beaten her. She was busy practising as JJ-Molly.

Samuel was hoping to jump into Tony's position as someone who went after the crowns. But Jamie had other plans. He shifted Jonah into Tony's vacant place and got Samuel to stay back at home base with Sheva.

As the first practice round started up, things didn't go well. Jamie was eliminated almost immediately. Jonah fell off the bridge and lost the one crown he'd grabbed. Even Molly was struggling to keep the attackers out of the fort.

By the time their fort had been raided, there were far too many bandits for Sheva and Samuel to keep away from their crown. They watched helplessly as their opponents racked up win after win.

"We need to try something different," Samuel suggested through his headset. "They get across the bridge too easily."

"Right," Jamie said. "The new guy has it all sussed out."

New guy? Samuel thought. *Molly and I are the only veterans on the team!*

"We need to set traps and blow the bridges," Samuel said. "If they have no way to cross, they can't get to our crown."

"There's not enough time to build anything," Jonah blurted. "They'll be on us before we can get something together."

"You haven't seen Samuel at work," Molly said. "He's fast from years of practice."

Jamie jumped in. "No, we keep doing it this way until we get it right. The tournament is tomorrow. We don't have time to completely change everything now!"

As the next round started, Samuel shook his head and muted his mic. "We *need* to change everything," he whispered to himself as their team sprang into action.

*   *   *

The day of the esports tournament arrived, and Samuel arrived at the Midtown Bank Arena with butterflies in his stomach. There were lots of people walking around. Some of them were wearing matching shirts, announcing the name of their team.

Builder Boyz, Samuel thought, reading the white letters on their black shirts. *That's not much better than Jamie's Juggernauts.*

"Samuel!" a familiar voice called. "Over here!"

Samuel looked and saw Molly waving him over. She was standing with the rest of the JJ crew.

"Mum didn't get a flat tyre this time, eh?" Molly said with a big smile.

Samuel shook his head. "No, but seeing this crowd, I kind of wish she had!"

Jamie looked up. "Glad you're here, Samuel. I think we're on . . . like, now!"

Before Samuel had a chance to even think, they were running towards one of the doorways leading into the arena.

*   *   *

As there were so many teams competing for the top spot, the rounds were single elimination. It they lost, they were out. For each match of CAPTURE THE CROWN played, only one team would move on to the next round and three others would be out.

The Juggernauts struggled in their first match. Samuel didn't see a bandit break up the ceiling above their fort. He was quickly taken out. Jamie and Sheva fell off the bridge while chasing someone who had taken their crown. Molly and Jonah were were up against the clock. The East and North forts were both eliminated with the score tied 1–1.

Samuel watched two members of the West team split off as Molly ran back towards their home base with their crown. One chased after Molly, while one grabbed the Juggernaut's South crown.

Jonah turned and ran at the other crown thief, knocking the player and himself into the void. Molly ran into the Juggernaut's South Fort with the West crown. She scored their first victory.

"That was way too close," Samuel said.

"We've got this," Jamie said. "On to the next round!"

CHAPTER 10

BUILDING A WIN

Jamie's Juggernauts squeaked by with a string of wins. As the competition grew, each victory was just a little more difficult to achieve than the last one. Samuel didn't like their strategy and thought they could win much more easily. But, as the captain and team's namesake, Jamie insisted.

"We're doing something right," Jamie bragged. "We're in the finals!" If they won their last match, they would represent Ohio and compete against the other 49 winning teams across the United States.

The tournament bracket displayed the final four teams. Jamie's Juggernauts were set to compete against Top of the Topia, Fort Wrecker 5 and Builder Boyz.

Nothing was working. Almost immediately, Jamie and Jonah were eliminated. Samuel glanced over to his teammates to see Jamie tear off his headset and throw it down on the keyboard. Jonah held his face in his hands. The only advantage they had was the entire South team was eliminated.

"Just the three of us left, West squad," Sheva spoke into her mic. "What's the plan?"

"Molly, can you keep them busy?" Samuel asked. "I've got some building to do."

"Got it," Molly shouted. She leapt across the bridge and knocked an opponent or two into the abyss.

"I'll keep them off your back, Samuel!" Sheva cried. She fired arrows as opponents advanced on their West fort.

Moving quickly, Samuel laid out the blue energy wiring to each of the two bridges that lead to their fort. He ran to one of them and built an extension out into the void. However, he left one small piece of wood hanging in the middle of nowhere and deleted the extension.

"What are you doing?" Sheva shouted. "You're building and deleting stuff? We're running out of time!"

"Trust him," Molly shouted. "He knows what he's doing!"

Samuel dodged a volley of arrows and ran back to the bridge to connect his switch.

In the next moment, he heard Sheva cry out. "They got me and the crown, guys!" She was out of the competition. "They're trying to bring our crown back to their base!"

With zero points on the board, East would grab the lead and eliminate Samuel's team if they returned their crown to the base and the other crowns stayed put.

"Molly," Samuel shouted. "I'm going in!"

"I'll go after our crown," she replied. "If I don't stop them, we're done!"

"North just scored South's crown," Jonah shouted. "It's 1–0. We need a miracle here!"

Samuel ran to the North fort, deleted their back wall, and snatched the crown before anyone could react. He moved to the East fort, leapt over their defender and landed on their roof. He quickly hammered through and dropped into the East crown room.

"Two crowns!" Samuel cried, grabbing the East's treasure.

He glanced at the time. There were fifteen seconds left. It was going to be close.

Samuel smacked a defender and deleted the ground beneath the opponent, dropping him into the void. Then he turned and built a quick wall to block their entrance before creating his own exit.

With seven seconds left, Samuel leapt

through the wall he'd destroyed to see five opponents from the remaining teams coming at him. With no time to spare, he ran to his rigged bridge.

"C'mon, c'mon!" Samuel cried. The players from North and East were hot on his tail. As he crossed the bridge, he tapped the switch and leaped out into the middle of the field.

"No!" he heard Jamie shout.

As the opponents followed him, the entire bridge blew up while Samuel was in midair. He could hear the crowd cheer as all the opponents dropped. Samuel landed expertly on his single block, suspended in midair.

Three seconds left . . .

Samuel did a jumbo jump towards their fort. The entire crowd gasped. It didn't look like he was going to make the landing.

But he did. Samuel Finnegan crossed the entrance of their fort with two crowns in his hand as the timer went off and signalled the game's end. The entire crowd erupted in a chorus of cheers and applause. Jamie's Juggernauts were going to the nationals!

After the crowds thinned out and people sifted out of the arena, Samuel walked out with the rest of the team.

"Nice work out there, Samuel," Jamie said. "I have to hand it to you, buddy. You know what you're doing."

"I was like, what is he doing out there?" Sheva said. "I had no idea what you were up to."

"Just building stuff, guys," Samuel said. "It's the whole point of the game, you know?"

"I think you could teach us a few things," Jamie said.

"Sure, I can do that," Samuel replied, then smiled. "On one condition. We have *got* to change the name of our team."

MORE ABOUT WORLD-BUILDING GAMES

- *Buildtopia* is a fictional world-building game, similar to *Minecraft*. *Minecraft* is the best-selling video game of all time. Released on 18 November 2011, it was originally free to play online. As of 2023, it has gone on to sell over 300 million copies!

- The game that inspired *Minecraft* was *Infiniminer*. It was created in 2009, two-and-a-half years before *Minecraft*. Like *Minecraft*, it had a "blocky" look and allowed players to dig and build their own worlds.

- *Roblox* is a game where you can build your own worlds and visit worlds that others have designed. It was released on 1 September 2006. Unlike earlier versions of *Minecraft*, *Roblox* focuses on online cooperation with other players.

- *Minecraft* introduced PvP (Player versus Player) online servers in 2011. This allowed players to build worlds and arenas to compete against each other in online battles.

MORE ABOUT ESPORTS

- The first esports competition took place at Stanford University in the United States in October 1972. Students there competed in a game called *Spacewar*. The grand prize was a year-long subscription to *Rolling Stone* magazine.

- There were over 532 million people watching esports events in 2023.

- Esports teams usually practise together for eight hours a day, seven days a week. That's longer than a 40-hour-a-week, full-time job. Many players practise on their own on top of that.

- A research study showed that during esports competitions, players had heart rates around 160–180 beats per minute. That's the equivalent of running as fast as you can!

- The best competitors get physical exercise to train their body and mind and sharpen their reflexes. Stretching and upper-body exercises help keep esports athletes healthy.

TALK ABOUT IT

1. Samuel loves the game *Buildtopia* and doesn't care if any of his friends or younger brother like it. Why do you think he likes the game so much? Do you have an interest in something that's considered unpopular with your friends and family?

2. When Samuel tried to get to the esports trials for Jamie's team, his mum got a flat tyre. He knew he could make it in time if he ran the rest of the way, but he didn't. Do you think he should have? Did Samuel make the right choice in staying to help his mum?

3. From the start, Samuel didn't like the team name "Jamie's Juggernauts". Why do you think that is? What stopped others on the team from saying how they felt about the name?

WRITE ABOUT IT

1. Samuel could've started his own team but didn't. Write about what might have happened if Samuel had put together his own *Buildtopia* squad. How would they have done against Jamie's Juggernauts? What do you think Samuel would've called his team?

2. Although Samuel was good at the CAPTURE THE CROWN update, he couldn't seem to beat The Architect at first. We later find out The Architect is Molly. Write a scene where Samuel and Molly play *Buildtopia* together for the first time. Does he show her his beloved Finnegan Castle? Do they exchange gaming secrets and building techniques?

3. Write the next chapter in the story with the team competing against the other 49 state champions. How will they do? Will Samuel's training for the other members of the team pay off?

GLOSSARY

broadcast send out by radio, television or internet for an audience to hear or watch

chasm deep opening in the surface of a planet

ghoul evil being of legend that robs graves and eats dead bodies; a monster

juggernaut massive force that crushes whatever is in its path

mechanics way something works

monstrous unusually large or enormous

pedestal support or base for a column, statue or some other object

pixels small dots, lines or squares that make up a digital or video image

reroute send or direct something on or along a different route

scandal behaviour that is considered wrong and causes a negative reaction from others

void empty space

ABOUT THE AUTHOR

Thomas Kingsley Troupe is the author of over 200 books for young readers. He's written books about everything from school werewolves to talking spaceships to ballerinas. Thomas wrote his first book when he was at primary school and has been making up stories ever since. When he's not behind the keyboard, he enjoys reading, playing video games and hunting ghosts with the Twin Cities Paranormal Society in Minnesota, USA. Otherwise, he's probably having a nap or something. Also, he loves cookies. Thomas lives in Woodbury, Minnesota, with his two sons.

ABOUT THE ILLUSTRATOR

Alan Brown is a freelance illustrator who has created artwork for Disney, Warner Bros. and the BBC, while continuing to provide illustrations for children's books and comics. Alan has worked mainly on children's books for those who find it hard to engage and be enthusiastic about reading. These clients include Harper Collins, Ransom, Franklin Watts and Ben 10 Omniverse.